Conte

Introduction

The concepts of time and money are often very difficult for children to understand, particularly when they are first introduced to them. This book has been written to support the work practitioners are doing with children in the Early Years Foundation Stage, and particularly during the Reception year.

The activities all use familiar and well established early years practice and resources to explore time and money in real life and imaginary situations through games, songs, role play and drama, and most of these activities can be planned for indoor or outdoor areas in early years settings.

The concepts of time and money are included within the Problem Solving, Reasoning and Numeracy (PSRN) area of learning in the Early Years Foundation Stage (EYFS), where the emphasis is on practical, first-hand experiences, open-ended activities and opportunities for children to extend and consolidate their learning through play and self-initiated activity.

Children need plenty of early experience in free play with the resources for time and money - toy or replica money, purses and watches can supply this experience, particularly in the very early stages of the EYFS.

However, real money, real clocks, real shopping with real bags, real experiences of time passing and spending money will be far more effective in helping children to understand how time and money work. Providing experiences of shopping, using real money, supplying real purses, bags and wallets, real watches and clocks, and drawing children's attention to day and night, the seasons and the passing of time will gradually build up their knowledge and understanding.

Resourceful practitioners will find ways of providing these real life experiences by scouring charity shops, requesting unwanted articles from families and friends, and using the environment around their setting to enrich children's experiences. Problem Solving, Reasoning and Numeracy are vital skills for lifelong learning, and a secure base to thinking is laid down in the playful activities of early childhood.

The Little Book of Time and Money

Supporting Problem Solving, Reasoning and Numeracy

By Dawn Roper

Illustrated by Martha Hardy

Published 2008 by A&C Black Publishers Limited
38 Soho Square, London W1D 3HB
www.acblack.com

ISBN 978-1-9060-2961-6

Text © Dawn Roper 2008
Illustrations © Martha Hardy 2008
Series Editor Sally Featherstone
A CIP record for this publication is available from the British Library.

Printed in Great Britain by Latimer Trend & Company Limited

This book is produced using paper that is made from wood grown in
managed, sustainable forests. It is natural, renewable and recyclable.
The logging and manufacturing processes conform to the environmental
regulations of the country of origin.

To see our full range of titles
visit **www.acblack.com**

All the activities in this book:

- are practical and easy to do;
- are carefully planned to help children make progress towards the Early Learning Goals for the EYFS;
- extend to other areas of learning;
- use familiar, cost-effective or free resources;
- have clear instructions.

By including some of these activities in your regular planning, you will help children to:

- develop a range of speaking and listening skills;
- form relationships with their peers and adults;
- develop their concepts of time and money in different situations.

Using the book

The activities in the book can be used in any order to support and develop a focused approach to the concepts of time and money, or as an informal resource for use with younger children.

Remember to be sensitive to the needs and beliefs of the children within your setting. Some younger children may not fully understand the difficult concepts of time and money, but they will enjoy joining in with the activities anyway. Enjoyment and play are essential initial stages in understanding a topic or reinforcing a concept.

The Mulberry Bush

A new version of an old song

What you need:
* a big space, indoors or outside

Key words:
* sing
* circle
* day
* breakfast time
* morning
* lunch time
* afternoon
* dinner time
* evening
* bed time
* night

Preparation:

Learn the song 'Here we go round the Mulberry Bush'.

Chorus

Here we go round the mulberry bush
The mulberry bush, the mulberry bush
Here we go round the mulberry bush
So early in the morning

Verse

This is the way we **brush our teeth**
Brush our teeth, brush our teeth
This is the way we **brush our teeth**
So early in the morning

The Activity:

1. Gather the children in a large enough area to move in a circle. Tell them you are going to sing a song together to help them learn about their day.
2. Sing the song with the children standing in a circle, skipping round together, holding hands then doing an action such as brushing their teeth.
3. Talk with the children about different things <u>they</u> might do in their day, such as getting dressed, playing with a brother or sister, going to the park, getting themselves ready for bed.
4. Now change the verse of the song to include something the children would do in the afternoon, such as '...play some games'.
5. Ask the children to suggest activities for different times of the day and include these in the song. What actions could they do for their ideas? Change some of the words of the song to say '...just before our bedtime' or '...when we have our snack time'.
6. For the chorus the children could do the actions for the verse instead of skipping round in a circle. Younger children could jump on the spot or dance round a marker. Older children could jump up and down while singing the verse in time to the beat.
7. Are there some things the children don't do every day? Discuss these and maybe you could incorporate them in a new version of the song, using '...every Sunday morning' or '...every Friday evening'. Talk about the difference between 'every day' and 'every Friday'.

and another idea ...

* Invite the adults in the setting to join in with the verse, putting things in that <u>they</u> do in their day.
* Record the children singing on a tape recorder and play it back to them.

Links with the Early Learning Goals

CD: Use language to imagine and recreate roles and experiences.
CD: Form good relationships with adults and peers.

What's the Time Mr Wolf?

An enjoyable and collaborative time game to play together

What you need:
* a large clock or clock face
* a space outdoors

Key words:
* clock
* hands
* time
* o'clock
* numbers
* 1-9
* What time is it?

Preparation:

Do plenty of practice at recognising the numbers from 1-12 in counting and as numerals. Get involved in counting forwards and backwards from 0. Make or find a big clock face with moving hands and clear numerals.

The Activity:

1. Go outside into a big space with the children.

2. Show the children how to play 'What's the Time Mr Wolf?' with an adult as the wolf. The wolf stands facing a wall or fence, and the children stand facing the wolf's back. They say 'What's the Time Mr Wolf?' and the wolf says a time (eg '2 o'clock'). The children take that many steps towards the wolf. When the wolf says 'Dinner time!' and turns to chase the children, they run away to a safe spot (eg a chalk circle). If the wolf catches a child before they get to the safe spot, they become the wolf.

3. When the children know the game, you can use a clock face to help with learning the time. Stand next to the child who is being the wolf and when the other children say 'What's the Time Mr Wolf?' show the wolf a time on the clock and the wolf must say what time it is. Start at any hour, then when the clock is at 12 o'clock, it is the wolf's dinner time, and the wolf can chase the children and hopefully catch one.

4. For a change, put pictures at appropriate times on the clock (8 o'clock for breakfast, 5 o'clock for tea, 7 o'clock for bed time) and the wolf could shout 'Breakfast time!', 'Tea time!' or 'Bed time!' at the appropriate time.

5. Read 'What's the Time Mr Wolf?' by Colin Hawkins or 'What's the Time Mr Wolf?' by Annie Kubler. These story books are both good vehicles for games and role play as well as giving good opportunities for practising telling the time. Each could be the basis for a session out of doors or inside, and the illustrations will inspire talk, drawing, painting and counting.

and another idea ...

* Make giant clocks with the children so they can then play the game independently and at different times of the day.
* Go on a clock hunt around your setting. How many clocks and watches can the children find?

Links with the Early Learning Goals

PSRN: Recognise numerals 1 to 9.
PD: Show awareness of space, of themselves and others.

Hickory Dickory Dock

A rhyme about clocks

What you need:
* indoor or outdoor spaces
* large, empty cardboard boxes

Key words:
* time
* clock
* numbers
* 1-12
* listen
* rhyme
* song

The Little Book of Time and Money

Preparation:

Learn this nursery rhyme as a basis for actions and counting as the children reinforce time telling.

Hickory, dickory dock
The mouse ran up the clock
The clock struck one
The mouse ran down
Hickory dickory dock
Tick tock Tick tock

...The clock struck two
What will the mouse do?
...The clock struck three
The mouse could see.
...The clock struck four
The mouse ran to the door.

The Activity:

1. Sing the song together, encouraging the children to run their fingers up their arms for the mouse, and showing the right number of fingers for the number that the clock is chiming.
2. Work with the children to create their own grandfather clock using cardboard boxes. Paint the clock and make some moving hands for the face.
3. When the children have practised the rhyme, they can then start to use numerals to show the number the clock is chiming.
4. Help the children to think of other verses for the different numbers. Do not insist, especially for younger children, that the words should rhyme. This can be worked on with the children later.
5. Now use your clock as you sing the song. Let individuals choose a time to place the clock hands. How many verses can you make together for the times chosen? Can you make up some actions?
6. Add some sticks or other simple musical instruments to make the 'tick-tock' of the clock as you sing and do the actions. Clap, slap or click your fingers as you sing. Or make yourselves into a huge clock by joining together to make a big circle with one child in the middle as the clock hands, moving and stopping.

and another idea ...

* You could make some simple number stickers from 1-12 for the children to wear, and play a race game, getting into a circle in the right order for a clock face. They may need some practice!

Links with the Early Learning Goals

CD: Recognise and explore how sounds can be changed, sing simple songs from memory, recognise repeated sounds and sound patterns and match movements to music.

CD: Listen with enjoyment, and respond to stories, songs, music.

Can we Clock in? Yes we Can!

Make clocking-in cards or a book for a builders' yard role play

<table>
<tr><td>

What you need:
* role play resources
* clocking-in cards or a book
  with pictures and names
* a big clock face or a clock
* pictures of builders' yards or
  construction sites

</td><td>

Key words:
* clock in
* time
* hours
* clock out
* start

</td><td>

* finish
* pay
* count
* overtime
* shift
* tea break

</td></tr>
</table>

Preparation:

Set up your role play area, making the focus suitable for clocking-in - a builders' yard, a factory, a hospital or a place where people work in shifts. You could make clocking-in cards or a clocking-in book for shift workers. Make some clocking-in cards with the children, adding a small drawing or photo to each. You could buy a visitors' book to personalise with your group and include a setting name or the name of the role play area.

The Activity:

1. Talk about the sorts of work where people have to sign in or 'clock in', and why workers have to do this. The children may know about this from their parents and relatives. Decide what sort of role play you are going to set up. Many children (especially boys) would enjoy a builders' yard, but a hospital, factory, clinic or shop might be a good alternative.

2. Let the children collect the equipment they need and arrange the area.

3. Now talk about how the children will record the time they arrive at the area and when they leave. You can use:
    * a real analogue clock (get a cheap one from a pound shop)
    * a cheap digital clock (this is easier for children to record)
    * a card clock face (where you can change the hands yourself).

4. Make a place for keeping the clocking-in cards - a simple box, Velcro dots on a board, or slots in a piece of thick card.

5. The children can record when they join and leave the play:
    * with a clock stamp
    * by drawing the clock face
    * by writing the time

6. A child could stand by the entrance to the role play area and stamp a clock on each card as workers arrive and leave. The workers could draw the hands at the correct time and return the card to the box or board.

and another idea ...

* Add some relevant books and jigsaws to the role play area so the children can find more information.
* Make a design book with the children for photos and drawings of the constructions they make and equipment they use.

Links with the Early Learning Goals

PSRN: Use language such as 'greater', 'smaller', 'heavier' or 'lighter' to compare quantities.

PSRN: Say and use number names in order in familiar contexts.

CLL: Use language to imagine and recreate roles and experiences.

Dig, Dig, Digging

Excavating the past

What you need:
* objects in use today and older items - collect a good range of objects to bury and explore
* different sized paint brushes
* magnifying glasses, trowels

Key words:
* dig
* past
* present
* old
* new
* excavate
* archaeologist
* uncover
* buried
* treasure

Preparation:

Collect lots of different objects from the past and present that will help children to explore different periods of time. Ask other adults or the children's older relatives to see if they can help. Make sure that these objects are not of sentimental or monetary value as they may get broken.

Prepare a place for digging, burying and excavating. This could be a tray or big bowl of compost or sand, a grow bag, a patch of soil in your garden, or a pile of bark and leaves. Don't bury objects too far into the ground, as the children may struggle to get them out, and leave some of the objects partially hidden to add to the sense of excitement.

The Activity:

1. Talk with the children about how to find things out about the past and how lots of people have dug up objects to find out more. Remind them of the story of Indiana Jones.

2. Show the children the area you have created for digging up objects to find out more about the past.

3. Look together at the tools you are suggesting, and talk about how to use them in an excavation or 'dig'.

4. Talk about how they should be very careful when they find an object, using brushes and magnifying glasses to make sure they don't break or damage it as they uncover it. Offer a clean place - a piece of fabric, a tray or shallow box with compartments.

5. As they find more objects, encourage the children to look at each one through a magnifying glass so they can investigate what they have found. Do they think the object is old or new? How do they know?

6. Work together to make a museum or exhibition of your objects. You can write and draw labels and descriptions to make it like a real museum. If the children don't know what a museum is like, use Google and the internet to find pictures and museum sites.

and another idea ...

* Create a treasure map for the children with clues or labels to help them find the treasures.
* Use very small objects such as beads and coins to make a mini-dig, and use teaspoons and small brushes to excavate.

Links with the Early Learning Goals

KUW: Find out about past and present events in their own lives, and in those of their family and other people they know.

CLL: Extend their vocabulary, exploring the meanings and sounds of new words.

Time is Running Out

Making and using sand timers

What you need:
* a big indoor or outdoor space
* skipping ropes, balls, beanbags, hoops, skittles etc
* equipment such as a climbing frame, slide or balance bar
* sand timers

Key words:
* time
* minute
* timer
* sand timer
* safe
* safety
* space
* exercise
* out of breath
* energy
* count

Preparation:

Find some big sand timers, or make them with plastic bottles and dry sand coloured with food colouring - see www.wikihow.com/Make-a-Sand-Timer-from-Recycled-Plastic-Bottles for instructions. Let the children help.

Collect some PE or games equipment in the outside area. Use equipment which the children are familiar with so they know how to use it safely. You may need extra adults to help with this activity, particularly for larger or more complicated equipment like the climbing frame or skipping ropes, or to intervene gently in disputes!

The Activity:

1. Go outside with the children and show them the selection of sand timers. Talk about how they work and look carefully at them together. Why do they think there are different amounts of sand in the timers? What could you use sand timers for?
2. Explain to the children that they are going to have some races against the sand timers. When the timer has run out, tell the children that you will say 'STOP!' and they must stop the activity straight away and return to a starting point. Talk with the children about keeping themselves safe throughout this activity by watching where they are going and being aware of other people near them.
3. Look at the equipment together and talk about the different sorts of movements children could time. Are they going to throw the ball up in the air and see how many times they can catch it, or throw and catch with a partner?
4. Talk with the children about keeping a count of how many times they have done something like throwing the beanbag. Give the children time to explore the equipment before using the timers to count and compete.
5. Now try doing these activities against the timers. Longer sand timers may be used for more difficult tasks eg the climbing frame. Change activities so they have had a go at the different races available.
6. Come together to compare the different scores and celebrate everyone's achievements.

and another idea ...

* Have an exercise day at your setting where all the adults can join in with special timed races using a variety of different timers such as stop watches.
* Try some simple exercises indoors if it is a rainy day.

Links with the Early Learning Goals

CLL: Use talk to organise sequence and clarify thinking, ideas, feelings and events.

PD: Move with control and co-ordination.

Monday, Tuesday, Wednesday

Use a rhyme to remember the days of the week

What you need:
* a small parachute
* a big space
* days of the week written on large flash cards

Key words:
* days of the week
* weekend
* week day
* next
* before
* yesterday
* tomorrow

The Little Book of Time and Money

Preparation:

Write the days of the week songs on large pieces of paper and display them on the wall. You could include some of the music notes so the children start to relate music and song together. Check whether the children know the original tunes.

The Activity:

Days of the Week

(to the tune of Frere Jacques!)
There are seven
There are seven
Days of the week
Days of the week
Sunday, Monday, Tuesday
Wednesday, Thursday, Friday
Saturday
Come and play!
OR

Thursday, Thursday,
Thursday, Thursday,
Morning, noon and night,
Morning, noon and night
Yesterday was Wednesday,
Tomorrow will be Friday,
Just can't wait! Just can't wait!
(change the day to practise order of the days)

(to the tune of London Bridge)
There are seven days in a week, days in a week, days in a week.
There are seven days in a week.
Can you name them?
Sunday, Monday, Tuesday,
Wednesday, Thursday, Friday, and
Saturday.
What is today?

(to the tune of 'Oh my Darling')
Sunday, Monday
Tuesday, Wednesday
Thursday, Friday, Saturday
Sunday, Monday
Tuesday, Wednesday
Thursday, Friday, Saturday

1. Children need plenty of practice of the words before they can begin to listen to and remember order of the days ...
2. Sing the songs as parachute songs, creating a rhythm by shaking the parachute gently in time to the song. Movement helps memory, so keeping the beat will really help.

and another idea ...

* Have the days of the week flashcards displayed in different places around the setting for the children to collect and put in order.
* Work with the children to make up their own songs about the days of the week and things they do on each day.

Links with the Early Learning Goals

CD: Recognise and explore how sounds can be changed, sing simple songs from memory, recognise repeated sounds and sound patterns and match movements to music.

PD: Move with control and coordination.

A Week of Seven Days

A week-long activity about your setting

What you need:
* a large space outdoors
* paper
* pencil crayons and felt tips

Key words:
* day
* seven days
* week
* collect
* draw

Preparation:

Talk with the children about the activities they do in their week. You could ask parents or carers to note down some of the activities their children do in a typical week so you have a starting point. Make some posters, one for each child, with the days of the week and spaces underneath for pictures.

The Activity:

1. Gather the children in a quiet area.
2. Discuss with the children the different activities they do during the week. If the children find it difficult to remember, use some of the information you have been given by parents and carers.
3. Encourage the children to talk with each other about their activities so they can have a short discussion with a friend, gaining different ideas about what they might do in their week. Do any of the children do the same things in the evenings or at weekends? Is it on the same day?
4. Explain some of the things you do in your own week to give the younger children some examples - going to the supermarket, going for a jog, having a takeaway.
5. Work with the children to draw pictures of themselves doing things and sticking them onto the correct poster for the day.
6. Talk with the children about the blank days on their poster. What do they think they will do on those days? Perhaps they can add those events as the days go by.
7. Each day, invite the children to draw their own picture of something they have done and help them to stick it onto their poster under the right day.
8. Remember to look at the days earlier in the week and talk about what they did before in the week and what they might do in the days coming up.
9. Collect together the children's pictures and make a book of the week with the children. Put the book in your book area.

and another idea ...

* The children could take turns to take home a digital camera to record some of the activities they might do such as going to dance class, going to the park, or visiting a relative.

Links with the Early Learning Goals

CD: Use their imagination in art and design, music, dance, role play and stories.

CLL: Interact with others, negotiating plans and activities and taking turns in conversation.

Yesterday, Today and Tomorrow

Make a calendar to help with the days of the week

What you need:
* card in different colours
* scissors
* felt tips and crayons
* collage materials
* examples of calendars

Key words:
* week
* names of days
* calendar
* yesterday
* today
* tomorrow

Preparation:

Make some labels for the days of the week with the children, so they each have their own set to stick on their calendar of their own week. You could photocopy days of the week to cut out; older children could make their own cards using felt pens or crayons.

Collect some different sorts of calendars to look at together. Try to get different sizes and types. It's a good idea to start this activity on a Monday!

The Activity:

1. Gather the children in a quiet area and look at some examples of calendars together.
2. Explain that some people find calendars useful to help them to remember when to do things or record the things they have done.
3. Ask the children about things they did yesterday to check their understanding of the word. Explain that 'yesterday' is something they have already done, and is in the past.
4. Now do the same for the word 'tomorrow' and explain that this is something they are going to do in the future but they have not done it yet.
5. Talk with the children about making their own calendar of their week, starting with Monday and ending on Sunday.
6. Look together at the selection of art materials they can choose to use as they create their own calendar for a week using the large pieces of card.
7. Help the children to stick on the days of the week that you or the children have made together.
8. As the day progresses, the children can draw pictures and write words on their calendar as they complete their everyday activities in the setting. Some children may need reminding and all will need encouraging to keep up their concentration as the day goes by.
9. At the end of the day, compare some of the activities in which the children have been involved in.

and another idea ...

* Encourage the children to fill in what they do at home or with their parent or carer at the beginning of the session each day.
* Ask some of the adults in the setting to make their own weekly calendar for the children to see.

Links with the Early Learning Goals

CD: Express and communicate their thoughts and feelings by using a widening range of materials.

KUW: Find out about past and present events in their own lives, and in those of their families and other people they know.

January, February

Songs for the months

What you need:
* a big space
* some simple instruments to accompany the songs

Key words:
* month
* months
* year
* twelve
* first, second
* names of each month

Preparation:

Sing songs about time, days of the week, and months of the year. Practise these out of doors where you can look at the weather and seasons, as well as inside.

> *(To the tune and movements of 'The Macarena')*
> January, February, March and April,
> May, June, July and August,
> September, October, November, December,
> Hey, months of the year!

The Activity:

1. This song is a good way to start learning the months of the year, and as it has movements too, it is easier to learn and remember.
2. Once the children have learned this version, you can try all sorts of tunes and rhythms for making your own songs and rhymes for days of the week and months of the year.
3. You could try using a word for each month that helps them to remember , such as January-cold, August-seaside.
4. Use the song to make a months of the year interactive display with the children. Put the names of the months on a display board. Scribe some of the things the children do in each month and help them to put these into speech bubbles with a picture of the activity. Try removing the words or the pictures and see if the children can replace them in the right places.
5. Make a months book with the children. Use a double page spread for each month and collect pictures and events for every month. If children take this book home, they can add events that are important to their families, such as holidays, birthdays, celebrations and so on.
6. Provide diaries and calendars in role play and writing areas, such as homes, hairdressers, car maintenance workshops, DIY and builders' offices, travel agents, vets' and doctors' and dentists' surgeries.

and another idea ...

* Use stories and songs to help reinforce these sequences. Collect new versions from friends, families and colleagues. Try to get some in other languages. Make a days and months rhyme and song book for your setting.

Links with the Early Learning Goals

CLL: Listen with enjoyment, and respond to stories, songs and other music, rhymes and poems and make up their own stories, songs, rhymes and poems.

PSED: Form good relationships with adults and peers.

Tick, Tock, Look at a Clock

Investigating different sorts of clocks and watches

What you need:
* a selection of different clocks, watches and stop watches
* magnifying glasses
* small screwdrivers

Key words:
* clock
* watch
* hands
* work
* time
* stop watch
* tick
* hour
* minute
* second
* number

Preparation:

Collect a range of different sized and shaped analogue and digital clocks and watches and put them in an interesting box. Try charity shops, car boot sales, or by asking parents for clocks that are NOT digital. Check that all the clocks and watches the children are looking at are safe and do not have sharp edges or small pieces that could be swallowed.

The Activity:

1. Gather the children on a carpeted or quiet area.
2. Look at the 'treasure' box together. What do the children think might be inside the box?
3. Take turns to carefully take the objects out of the box and put them on the floor.
4. Talk with the children about what they think these objects are used for. How are they different from each other? Can the children sort or group them?
5. In small groups ask the children to investigate, looking closely at the clocks and watches using the magnifying glasses. What can they find out about the time pieces? What do the clocks look like when you use the magnifying glass?
6. Help the children to investigate how watches might work by taking the backs off, or dismantling them, using small screwdrivers. Look at all the pieces with magnifying glasses.
7. Ask the children 'Why do some of the clocks have plugs?' Discuss the differences between digital and analogue clocks and watches. Talk about what alarm clocks and timers do.
8. Make a collection of pictures of watches and clocks from catalogues. Look up these words on Google Images - 'clock', 'clock works', 'Big Ben', 'watch', 'digital clock' and 'grandfather clock' for some great pictures of the insides and outsides of clocks and watches.

and another idea ...

* Make a clock display for the children to investigate the differences between the time pieces.
* Enlarge close up photographs of clocks and watches so the children can investigate how the pieces fit together.

Links with the Early Learning Goals

CD: Find out about and identify the uses of everyday technology and use information and communication technology.

CD: Ask questions about why things happen and how things work.

The Clock Makers

Making clocks for a role play shop

Preparation:

Gather the children together and talk about how you could make a watch and clock shop. Collect lots of recycled materials to make things to sell, or ask parents and search charity shops for clocks and watches. Find examples of different watches and clocks. Send for some watch and clock catalogues or download information and pictures from the internet.

The Activity:

1. Decide where the shop will be and help the children to collect the furniture and objects they need. Real money leads to much more purposeful play, but make sure the children know how to check it's all back at the end of the game.

2. Set up a workshop area where the children can make their own watches and clocks to sell in the shop. As the children work, help them to overcome the difficulties of fastenings and straps as well as putting faces on clocks, making hands that go round, and getting them to stand up. Paper fasteners, elastic, hair scrunchies and masking tape may help. Tall square and rectangular boxes make good clocks, and making the face is good practice for time telling. Experiment with making packaging and boxes for watches. (You may be able to get unwanted watch boxes or other packaging from parents and friends.)

3. Make some posters and a catalogue of watches and clocks by using magazines, catalogues, photos of the clocks the children make, or pictures from the internet. Set out the shop with all the watches and clocks.

4. Make price tags and find some bags and wrapping materials, including gift wrap and ribbon.

5. Spread a piece of fabric on the counter so the watches can be displayed.

6. Make a big sign for the shop and hang it from the ceiling, and an OPEN/CLOSED sign for the door or table.

7. Now the shop is ready, children can take turns to be shopkeeper and customers, and even a watch or clock repairer.

and another idea ...

* Do some observational drawings of the clocks with the children. Display these pictures around the shop, or in the catalogue. Older children could create their own captions and labels for the drawings.

Links with the Early Learning Goals

CD: Explore colour, texture, shape, form and space in two or three dimensions.

PSRN: Count reliably up to ten everyday objects.

What Can You Find?

Find something old at home and bring it for the museum

What you need:
* card, pens, scissors for labels
* interesting or unusual objects
* fabrics such as voile or silk for drapes and display
* camera

Key words:
* object
* old
* new
* museum
* special
* look at
* visit
* ticket
* visitor
* curator
* display

The Little Book of Time and Money

Preparation:

Defining an old object is sometimes difficult, and 'old' does not just mean 'worn out'. What seems old to the children may not seem so to adults! Encourage children to think about things that were used before they were born.

Encourage children to look for old objects in charity shops and rummage or car boot sales. Old objects can also be found on beaches or when out walking. Check that the objects don't belong to anyone else and that they are not dangerous!

Write some letters to ask parents if children can bring objects that would have been used in the past for a class museum. Make sure parents know that the children will be looking and using the objects, so they don't send anything of sentimental or monetary value. Children love looking for treasure.

Try to get a children's metal detector and have a go at finding things in your outside area or at the park.

The Activity:

1. Sit with the children in a circle on the carpet and put their objects in the middle where everyone can see them. This also helps if some children have not been able to bring something.
2. Thank the children for taking their letters home and bringing special objects for everyone to look at. Talk with the children about handling special objects carefully to make sure they are respected and not damaged.
3. Now let the children introduce the objects they have brought and pass them carefully round the circle.
4. Discuss each object and whether the children think it is old or not.
5. Now talk about how you could make a museum for all the old objects you have talked about. Encourage the children to suggest where the museum should be and what it needs. Use the internet to get ideas.
6. The children can be curators of the museum, or make and sell tickets, postcards (made from digital photos of the exhibits) and souvenirs such as decorated pencils, old coins etc in the museum shop.

and another idea ...

* Visit your local museum for information and ideas. You could ask the museum education staff to visit your museum. They might even lend you some objects or artefacts to show.

Links with the Early Learning Goals

PD: Handle tools, objects, constructions and malleable materials safely and with increasing control.

CLL: Use language to imagine and recreate roles and experiences.

Clock Bingo

A simple bingo game to help with time recognition

What you need:
* bingo cards
* a large cardboard clock face
* counters
* somewhere quiet to play

Key words:
* time
* clock
* hands
* o'clock
* number
* hour
* half hour
* winner

The Little Book of Time and Money

Preparation:

Work with the children to make some clock bingo cards and a big clock face. You could try www.sparklebox2.co.uk for a free download if you need some help. Make sure the children recognise numbers 1-12 so they can match these numbers on the clocks later.

Start with analogue or digital clock faces showing hours only. You can add half hours later. Many children are more used to digital clock 'faces' so you may want to start with digital clock Bingo and move on to analogue clocks when children have mastered the analogue face. www.sparklebox2.co.uk offer a free download of digital clock Bingo. You will need to make a digital clock for the caller, or have a set of cards for them to hold up.

Start with hours and only have six clocks on each card.

The Activity:

1. When you play the game, sit in a quiet area with a small group of children.
2. Look at the large clock with the children.
3. Show the children the clock bingo cards and look at the different numbers on them. What numbers can they recognise? Check that all the children can recognise the clocks.
4. Give each child a bingo card and explain how to play. When you show the children a time on the large clock, they are going to look at their own card to see if they have a clock saying the same time. If they have, they can cover it or put a counter on it.
5. The winner of the game is the one who fills their card first with the clock faces. They shout 'BINGO!'
6. When the children are used to the game a child could be the caller.
7. Children could make their own 'Our Day' bingo cards using drawings of what they do at different times of the day with a little clock at the right time - such as 8am, 12pm, 5pm.

and another idea ...

* Make some clock Snap cards using a clock stamp or download pictures from the internet. Play regular Snap or Pairs (put the cards face down and turn over two that match).

Links with the Early Learning Goals

PSRN: Use everyday words to describe position.

PSED: Work as part of a group or class, understanding codes of behaviour for groups of people, including adults and children, to work together harmoniously.

Time Capsules

Collect objects for different times of the day and make your own time capsule

What you need:
* items children and adults would use throughout the day - eg toothbrush, soap, cereal box, lunch box, sports kit, book, pyjamas, etc
* empty boxes, paper or card for labels, sellotape, collage materials

Key words:
* time
* day
* morning
* earlier
* wake up
* afternoon
* evening
* later

Preparation:
Collect a range of different sized and shaped cardboard boxes so they are ready for the children to use. Collect some objects that are clearly lined with times of day.

The Activity:
1. Put the objects on a table - you could include a cereal box, toothbrush and toothpaste, hairbrush, flannel and soap, cereal bowl, pyjamas, a blanket, lunch box, water bottle, juice carton, TV paper, night light, teddy, alarm clock, and story book.
2. Work with a small group so everyone can participate.
3. Sit together in a circle somewhere quiet inside or out of doors.
4. Talk with the children about how some people put special things in a box and hide or bury it for other people to find many years later. Explain the term 'time capsule' by describing how the objects are chosen to show what people did and liked in the past.
5. Look at the boxes together and talk about making some time capsules for different times of the day. Talk with the children about the times of day they know about such as morning, afternoon, evening and night-time.
6. Look through the objects together and discuss what they might be used for. Take suggestions for more objects or pictures you could include. Encourage the children to use all their senses when talking about the objects, looking at them and feeling them carefully. How would these items be used? What time of day would they be used?
7. Now make some 'time of day' capsule boxes by labelling some boxes for 'morning', 'afternoon', 'evening' and 'night'.
8. Work with the children to select objects for each capsule. You may need more than one of some items!
9. Children can then place the time capsules in different areas in the setting for other children to investigate and explore. The children could bring other objects or pictures to add to the time capsules.

and another idea ...

* Each child could make a little 'time of day picture' of something they like to do at a certain time of the day. Stick these all over the time capsules. Adults in the setting and parents could join in too!

Links with the Early Learning Goals

CD: Respond in a variety of ways to what they see, hear, smell, touch and feel.

KUW: Investigate objects and materials by using all of their senses as appropriate.

Morning, Noon and Night-time too

Use a parachute to help children to understand the progress of the day

What you need:
* a small parachute
* a big space
* card and felt pens

Key words:
* morning
* afternoon
* evening
* time
* night
* daytime
* night-time

Preparation:

Work with the children to make some time cards with picture clues and words of morning, afternoon, evening and night. If you are working with older children, you could add some other times, such as snack time, lunch time, teatime.

The Activity:

1. Talk about the 'time of day' cards; make sure the children know which is which.
2. Invite the children to think about things they might do in the morning, such as wake up or eat their breakfast, things they might do in the afternoon, the evening and at night. Are there any things that they might do in the morning that they do in the evening as well? For example, brush their teeth, have a shower or bath, or sleep.
3. Show the children the parachute and explain that you are going to play a time game using the 'time of day' cards they looked at earlier.
4. Spread the parachute out flat on the floor.
5. Choose four children to stand at equally spaced places round the parachute, holding the 'time of day' cards. Starting with 'morning' at the top of the parachute, and go round clockwise adding 'afternoon', 'evening' and 'night'.
6. The rest of the children stand near the parachute.
7. An adult (or a child, once they are used to the game) calls out an activity the children would do every day (such as 'have breakfast' or 'get dressed').
8. The children run to stand behind the child holding the correct card for the time of day they do this activity.

and another idea ...

* Make picture cards of activities such as brushing teeth, eating fruit, and getting dressed. Put these cards under the parachute. Lift it up and let the children take turns to crawl underneath the parachute, choose a card and run round the parachute to the right 'time of day' card.

Links with the Early Learning Goals

KUW: Show an awareness of change.
PSRN: Use everyday words to describe position.
CLL: Begin to make patterns in their experience by linking cause and effect, sequencing, ordering and grouping.

Let's Go Shopping!

role play shops with real money

What you need:
* a till and real or plastic money
* bags and wrapping paper
* card, pens, scissors for labels and prices
* shopkeeper outfits or badges
* baskets, bags and purses

Key words:
* money
* price
* how much?
* change
* cost
* customer
* shopkeeper
* wrap
* queue
* turn

Preparation:

Role play is one of the best ways to introduce work with money. Any role play that involves exchange of money is useful, and children love bags and purses for real or plastic money. Real money is much more effective in learning about coins, because it makes a sensory link with the real word.

Resources to collect
* empty cartons
* purses
* carrier bags
* shopping bags
* baskets

* backpacks
* wallets
* handbags
* old credit/loyalty cards
* gift boxes and bags
* wrapping paper

* gift ribbon
* tape
* till rolls
* small note pads
* card for menus/labels
* newspaper/pizza boxes

Situations

Food shops	Other shops	Services	Eating out
* corner shop	* newsagent	* Post Office	* cafe
* baker	* toy shop	* travel agent	* fish and chips
* greengrocer	* antique/junk shop	* optician	* takeaway pizza
* supermarket	* chemist	* hairdresser	* Chinese/Indian
* gift shop	* electrical shop	* garden centre	* Italian/Tapas

The Activity:

1. Make sure the children are as involved as possible in the preparation and organisation of the role play area. This way, they will be more involved in making it work. Don't provide all the resources at once - wait until they ask, then try to provide what they want.

2. Focus on the time and money aspects of this sort of role play, such as bills, receipts, change, counting, coin recognition, opening and closing times, menus suited to the time of day, paying the workers and waiters and so on.

3. Provide plenty of writing and mark-making materials.

---

and another idea ...

* Why not try something different, such as:
    Santa's Grotto
    a car wash
    an ice cream parlour
    a market stall
    a Christmas shop?

Links with the Early Learning Goals

CLL: Attempt writing for different purposes, using features of different forms such as lists, stories and instructions.

PSED: Form good relationships between adults and peers.

Five Currant Buns

paying and change with a familiar song

What you need:
* a large space to sing the rhyme and act it out
* real coins to pay
* an apron for the baker
* some buns, real if possible

Key words:
* sing
* rhyme
* pay
* coin
* change
* turn
* name
* spend

The Little Book of Time and Money

Preparation:

Make currant buns with the children so they can eat them when they have 'bought' them. The buns taste better if you eat them on the same day as you bake them!

The Activity:

For 18 buns you need:

100g/4oz butter or margarine
100g/4oz caster sugar
2 eggs lightly beaten
100g/4oz self-raising flour

75g/3oz raisins or currants
9 cherries cut in half
paper cases

1. Put 18 paper cases on a baking tray.
2. Cream the butter or margarine with the sugar until light and fluffy.
3. Beat in the eggs.
4. Fold in the flour and the currants using a metal spoon.
5. Divide the mixture between the paper cases.
6. Put half a cherry on each bun.
7. Bake in a moderately hot oven for 15-20 minutes.
8. Transfer to a wire rack and leave to cool.

The rhyme

> FIVE currant buns in a baker's shop
> Round and fat with a cherry on the top
> Along came (say child's name), with a penny one day
> Bought a currant bun and took it away.
> FOUR currant buns in a baker's shop... etc.

When the buns are cool, sing the song together until everyone (including the baker) has one. Eat and enjoy!

Older or more experienced children might like to choose how much to pay for their bun, or may even need change.

and another idea ...

* Make salt dough buns with the children. These will last longer so you can sing the rhyme again. Remind the children that these buns are not for eating and they will only keep for a couple of weeks.

Links with the Early Learning Goals

PSRN: Say and use number names in order in familiar contexts.

CD: Recognise and explore how sounds can be changed, sing simple songs from memory, recognise repeated sounds and sound patterns.

What Sort of Money?

Money sorting games

<table>
<tr><td>

What you need:
* coins
* hoops, rope or string circles
  or strong paper cut in circles
  for sorting
* a container for the coins

</td><td>

Key words:
* coin
* sort
* same
* different
* difference

</td><td>

* shape
* amount
* colour
* silver
* bronze
* golden

</td></tr>
</table>

The Little Book of Time and Money

Preparation:

It is important to use real money if at all possible. Collect lots of coins of small denominations (1p, 2p, 5p, 10p pieces) and have smaller numbers of the higher denominations (50p, pound and two pound coins). Banks will provide you with change and may be able to give you new coins for a more exciting experience. Put the coins in a big bag or tin.

The Activity:

1. Sit with the children in a quiet area indoors or even outside.
2. Pour the coins out into a space on the carpet and spread them out. Look at all the coins together, feel them, smell them, listen to the way they sound when you rattle them together.
3. Talk about the different coins, naming the shapes and colours of each. Can the children find numbers on the coins? Can they find coins of the same shape, but different sizes?
4. Now show the children the hoops, rings or strings you have made. Show them how to sort the coins - you could perhaps sort by colour first.
5. Now see if the children can think of another way of sorting the coins. They may suggest sorting coins of the same shape, such as circles. Each time the sorting is completed, and all the coins are sorted, talk about the numbers of coins, using 'more', 'less', 'bigger', 'smaller', 'same', 'different'. Put the coins together that the children think have something in common and discuss their properties with the children. Why are they the same?
6. Now find some ways of making patterns with the coins. Which coins fit together without leaving spaces? Which coins are best for making flowers? Or wheels? Or faces?
7. Try piling coins in towers of five and ten to practise counting. Which coins are easiest to stack? Can the children make a stack of 20?
8. Find some small plastic bags and sort the coins into these bags, like a bank cashier or shopkeeper.

and another idea ...

* Create a display to encourage the children to sort in different ways with sorting trays.
* Make labels with the children, using some of the words from the discussion eg silver, bronze, sides, corners, round, hexagon etc.

Links with the Early Learning Goals

PSRN: Talk about, recognise and recreate simple patterns.
KUW: Look closely at similarities, differences, patterns and change.

In my Purse or in my Pocket?

Money games and challenges with purses

What you need:
* a range of wallets and purses
* real coins
* a money bank or jar
* card, pens, scissors

Key words:
* money
* coins
* amount
* purse
* wallet
* how much?
* how many?
* together
* change
* give
* share

Preparation:

Collect a range of different purses and wallets made from different materials and put them in a special box by draping a cardboard or wooden box in some fabric. Put the purses and wallets in the box.

Decide on appropriate coins to use with the group of children. For most children, it's enough to have single penny pieces. More experienced children may be able to use a range, but don't go too fast as children need a lot of experience before they understand about 2p, 5p and 10p.

Sequence of using and understanding different coins

* 1p coins only
* 1p and 2p coins
* 1p, 2p, 5p coins
* 1p, 2p, 5p, 10p coins

Children who can understand and use these values by the end of the EYFS will be fine!

* 1p, 2p, 5p, 10p, 20p
* 1p, 2p, 5p, 10p, 20p, 50p
* 1p, 2p, 5p, 10p, 20p, 50p, £1

The Activity:

1. Sit with the children in a quiet area and show them the special box you have prepared. Ask them to think about what might be in the box.
2. Help the children to take out all the wallets and purses and spread them out on the floor. Take some time to look carefully at the purses and wallets and ask the children what they think about them. What do they look like? Encourage the children to feel them and choose the ones they like best.
3. Ask the children what they think they are for and introduce the words 'wallet' and 'purse'. Explain that men often choose to use wallets and women often choose to use purses, but not always!
4. Empty the money out onto the floor and work with the children to share out the coins so everyone has an equal amount. If there is some left over this can go back into the money box. Compare the quantity of coins the children have as they are sharing it out. Has everyone got the same? How do the children know?
5. Try playing a simple money matching game where the children must turn up a card, find the amount and put it in their purse. Make the cards by stamping or sticking the coins on a card and writing the amount in numbers.

and another idea ...

* Make your own cards with coin stamps, sticky coins or real coins for Money Bingo, Money Snap, or Money Pairs.
* Use small zip-lock bags to make counting and sorting bags for coins.

Links with the Early Learning Goals

PSRN: Use language such as 'greater', 'smaller,' 'heavier', or lighter to compare quantities.

KUW: Investigate objects and materials by using all of their senses as appropriate.

Drop a Penny, Make a Wish!

Make a wishing well

What you need:
* pictures of wishing wells
* a big cardboard box
* kitchen roll or gift wrap tubes
* paint, brushes, card, scissors
* real pennies, purses and wallets

Key words:
* cut
* make
* wishing well
* wish
* how many?
* souvenir
* postcard
* true
* pay
* ticket

Preparation:

Together, look at some photographs of wishing wells together. Explain to the children that people sometimes believe that if they throw a penny into the wishing well and make a wish, then their wish will come true. Explain that some wishing wells have water in them, some do not. You could put some foil at the bottom of your well so you can see and count the pennies, or you could even have a shallow container of real water.

Now work with the children to make the wishing well from cardboard boxes and tubes. Make the well as big as you can, so it is realistic and can really be used for role play. Use the computer and photographs of some wishing wells to create and print out some postcards to sell in the wishing well café.

The Activity:

1. Sit near the wishing well and talk with the children about wishes and the wishes they would like to come true.

2. Now talk about how the children might use their wishing well to make their own wishes.

3. Cut some small pieces of card for wishing cards. The children can draw or write their wishes on the cards and throw them into the well with a penny as they make a wish.

4. Help the children to count the pennies in the wishing well. How many wishes have been made today?

5. Make a café area with the children so they can have a drink after they have made a wish. They will need more coins to pay for their refreshments.

6. Make some signs and a menu to show people how much the different drinks and refreshments cost.

7. The children can take turns serving and taking the money in the wishing well café or being the customers. Don't forget to make some postcards and other souvenirs. You could even make some little wishing well models from clay or baked and painted dough.

and another idea ...

* Make a display using pictures of wishing wells from around the world. You could put a water tray in the display and float water lilies for a peaceful reflection area for the children to think about their wishes, using pennies to make the wishes.

Links with the Early Learning Goals

PSRN: Count reliably up to ten everyday objects.

PSED: Understand that people have different needs, views, cultures and beliefs, that need to be treated with respect.

CD: Explore colour, shape, form.

I Went to the Shops and I...

A memory circle game

What you need:
* a big piece of paper or flipchart
* felt tip
* strips of paper, pencils
* some example shopping lists

Key words:
* shops
* shopping list
* pay
* amount
* money
* buy
* need
* think
* remember
* receipt

Preparation:

Make sure the children know what a shopping list is. You could read the story 'Don't Forget the Bacon' which is about remembering a shopping list.

The Activity:

1. Sit with the children in a quiet area and explain to them that you are going to play a new game called 'I went to the shops'.

How to play

* Say (for example) 'I went to the shops and I bought an apple.'
* The child sitting next to you repeats what you have said and adds their own item eg 'I went to the shops and I bought an apple and a hair bobble.'
* The game continues round the circle with each child adding a new item to the end of the list.

2. Younger children could draw a picture of what they are buying on a shopping list card or a small whiteboard before passing it on to the next person. Older children can try to remember the list and say it.
3. Now spread out a large piece of paper on the floor and ask the children to remember the list of items they said in the game. The younger children can use their whiteboard or paper to help them remember. Write the items in a list on the piece of paper. Talk about the shopping list you have made.
4. Talk about the things that families buy in their typical weekly shopping eg bread, milk, vegetables. Discuss why we need these things. What else do we buy for our homes when we go shopping?
5. Let the children make their own shopping list of things they think they need in a week, using pictures, single letters and words.
6. Younger children could cut out pictures of the things they need and make a picture shopping list.
7. Now use the lists and some money to do some shopping in a role play shop.

and another idea...

* Encourage the children to make shopping lists at home with their families and bring them back into the setting to talk about.
* get in the habit of writing lists when you prepare for activities together.

Links with the Early Learning Goals

CLL: Know that print carries meaning and, in English, is read from left to right, and top to bottom.

PSED: Work as part of a group or class, taking turns and sharing fairly.

Toy Stories, Toy Shop

Have a charity toy sale

What you need:
* toys to sell
* a till
* real money
* card and pens for price labels

Key words:
* toy
* sale
* money
* coins
* donate
* charity
* gift
* want
* give
* buy

The Little Book of Time and Money

Preparation:

Talk to the children about charity shops and events. You could do this activity as part of Red Nose Day or another local or national charity event. Work with the children to decide which charity you want the money you all raise to go to. What interests the children? It might be children less fortunate than them in other countries, for a disaster that might have happened recently or maybe for a local hospice.

Help the children to write or draw pictures for a note to their family, and for some posters explaining you are having a toy sale to raise money for charity, and inviting them to donate suitable unwanted toys. Set a date and invite parents and carers to come.

The Activity:

1. Collect together all the unwanted toys and work with the children to get them ready for the sale. Talk with the children about how you could sort and display them - small soft toys, large soft toys, jigsaws, books etc.
2. Ask the children how much they think they should charge for the toys. Can they work out a fair way of pricing toys of different sizes, types and conditions.
3. Work with the children to make signs for the sale and price labels for different toys. Then spread the toys out so they look attractive and well organised.
4. Decide with the children who will be the shopkeepers. practice what the shopkeepers need to say and do.
5. When it is time for the sale, help the children to sell the toys to the customers, checking the money and giving change if needed.
6. When the sale is over, help the children to count all the money and work out how much money they have raised for their chosen charity.
7. Try to arrange for a representative from the charity to come to your setting to receive the money and thank the children.
8. What will you do with any left-over toys? Ask the children for ideas. Perhaps you could give them to a hospital or a charity shop.

and another idea ...	Links with the Early Learning Goals
* Take some photos of the toy sale and how the children organised it. You could use them to make a book and include the amount of money the children raised and which charity it was for.	PSRN: Use developing mathematical ideas and methods to solve practical problems. PSED: Work as part of a group or class, taking turns and sharing fairly.

Visit the Bank

Find out what happens in a real bank

What you need:
* some real coins
* paper and pens for thank you
  letters

Key words:
* bank
* money
* coins
* cashier
* safe
* manager
* cheque
* visit
* thank you
* ask
* account

Preparation:

Find out when would be an appropriate day and time to visit your local bank. Plan what you want the children to see and do on the visit - talk to the cashier, visit the office and talk to the bank manager, find out where all the money is kept.

Visit the bank in person before you take the children, so you know what to expect and the bank has some warning of the visit. Make sure you tell parents about the visit and get their permission.

The Activity:

1. Talk about the visit before you go. Explain what a bank is and how it works to keep people's money safe.
2. Tell the children you have arranged a visit to a bank to learn more about money. Find out if anyone has ever been to the bank with their family.
3. Explain to the children what will happen at the bank, and remind them about how to behave on a visit to a new place. Decide what the children will ask about, and who they would like to talk to.
4. Look at the outside of the building. What can the children see? Are there any posters or labels and captions in the window?
5. Look at the cash machine outside. What do the children think this is used for? Look at the different numbers on the machine. What numbers do the children recognise? Do they know how it works?
6. Walk inside the bank and explore the different things that customers might find there - paying-in envelopes, pens, payment slips and leaflets.
7. Look carefully at the counter and the cashiers. If the bank is not too busy, invite the children to pretend they are customers and talk to the cashiers.
8. If the manager or someone else from the bank is available to talk to the children, see what else they can find out about banks.
9. Go back to the setting and make a list or some pictures with the children of the different things they saw at the bank.
10. Remind the children to send some thank you letters.

and another idea ...

* Create a role play bank in your setting. Use dressing-up clothes and accessories such as hats and bags to help the children become different characters visiting the bank. Make some badges for the bank employees.

Links with the Early Learning Goals

CLL: Interact with others, negotiating plans and activities and taking turns in conversation.
PSRN: Say and use number names in order in familiar contexts.

The Little Book of Time and Money

Spend it on Your Holiday

Looking at foreign coins

Preparation:

Collect as many different foreign coins and notes as you can. It is more difficult now that we have the Euro, so ask parents, friends and colleagues to look for any they may have, and keep this collection so you can use it again. Don't forget to include the different UK versions of familiar coins.

The Activity:

1. Sit with the children in a circle and put the map and globe in the middle of the circle. Look at the globe and the map with the children. Ask them what they think these items are used for.
2. Some children may be able to explain that we use maps and globes to find where different countries are in the world. If not, you may have to explain, but give them a chance first.
3. Look at some countries the children may have visited, such as popular holiday destinations like Spain. Help the children to find Spain on the globe and the map.
4. Explain to the children that different countries sometimes use different coins from those we use in England. Tip some of these coins out on the carpet and let the children feel and look at them - give them plenty of time for this.
5. Can the children find any that look similar or some that match? Talk about the similarities and differences.
6. Put out some paper and crayons and show the children how to make rubbings of the coins they like. This is easier if you put some layers of newspaper on the table, then the coins, then some blank paper to crayon on. Press hard with the crayon - it's sometimes easier to use the side of the crayon.
7. Look carefully at the pictures and patterns that come through the paper.
8. You could cut out the rubbing to make collages and patterns or use the rubbing sheets to make a backing for a display of the foreign coins, maps and globe. You could add some postcards and photos of coins downloaded from the internet

and another idea ...

* Make a mobile by sticking some of the rubbings onto card and cutting them out. You could also hang some of the coins up if you use strong glue such as No More Nails or put them in little zip-lock bags.

Links with the Early Learning Goals

PD: Use a range of small and large equipment.
KUW: Look closely at similarities, differences, patterns and change.

Higher Prices

Introducing coins of higher denominations

What you need:
* 20p, 50p and £1 coins
* small items to sell (eg paper clips, strings of beads, plastic cups, Lego bricks, pasta shapes)
* a till, a table for a counter
* zip-lock bags

Key words:
* sell
* buy
* amount
* coin
* pound
* how much?
* change
* shop
* pay

The Little Book of Time and Money

Preparation:

Work with a group of children who are ready for higher value coins, and make sure they understand the differences between the individual coins. Talk about real shops and how much things cost.

The Activity:

1. Show he children the bags you have brought and suggest that they could use these to make a shop that sells bags of small items.
2. Talk about the sorts of things you have in your setting that could fit in the bags. You may want to give the children some ideas or show them some examples.
3. Work together to collect lots of small items such as paper clips, counters, beads, sequins, lentils, dried beans etc.
4. Talk about the concept of 1p for each item, so the bags will cost 20p, 50p, £1, depending on the number of items in the bag.
5. Decide how many of each item will go in each bag, and how much each bag will cost. Encourage the children to think and count in fives and tens. Some may like to count in 20s, 50s or even 100s.
6. When the bags are ready, help the children to put a label and price each one.
7. Prepare the shop counter or table, fill the till with higher denomination coins - 20p, 50p, £1, £2. Collect some purses or wallets for the customers.
8. Open your shop - some children will be customers, some will be the shop-keepers.
9. Help the children if they need it, but try to stand back and just watch what happens. You could observe what each child is showing you that they can do, so this is an ideal opportunity for some assessment.
10. As children get more used to higher prices and coins of higher denominations, give them plenty of opportunities to practice in play and in activities such as snack time or outdoor play, where you could ask them to pay with real or plastic coins for snack items or rides on wheeled toys.

and another idea ...

* Work with the children to make their own posters and labels for the shop.
* Make things to sell to parents and carers and have a shop where the children help to sell the items. These could be paintings or art and craft items.

Links with the Early Learning Goals

PSRN: Use developing mathematical ideas and methods to solve practical problems.

PSED: Form good relationships with adults and peers. Work as part of a group.

Play the Game

Some games to make and play

What you need:
* a small parachute
* a big space
* card and felt pens

Key words:
* morning
* afternoon
* evening
* time
* night
* daytime
* night-time

The Little Book of Time and Money

The Activity:

1. **Money Bingo**

   Use the downloads on www.sparklebox2.co.uk to make some Bingo cards and boards with coins on them. Or you could make your own with sticky coins or even real coins covered with sticky-backed plastic. Make the cards simple to start with - 1p coins only, with number cards for the caller.

2. **Money Snap or Pairs**

   Make some cards with groups of coins in different patterns and use them to play Snap or Pairs (where you put the cards face down and try to turn up matching values). Start with cards of 1p coins, then add 2p coins and so on as the children get used to the games.

3. **Guess my Coin**

   Take turns to choose a coin from a special box or bag (without the other players seeing it). The other players must ask you questions about the coin to find out which one you have chosen eg Is it silver? Is the coin round? The children then have to guess what they think the coin is.

4. **Guess How Much?**

   This game encourages children to estimate. Get some small zip-lock bags and put a few coins in each one. Close the bags. The children take turns in choosing a bag and estimating how much money is in it. When they have guessed, they can tip the money out and check to see if they were right.

5. **Money Grab**

   Put some coins in a 'feely bag' and make some cards with amounts such as 2p, 6p and 9p on them. Put the cards face down on the carpet or table. Children take turns to turn over a card and grab the correct money from the bag without looking. This is harder than it seems, so start with small amounts and only have pennies in the bag. You can make it more challenging later.

6. **Penny Winks**

   Play Tiddly Winks with penny coins and count up your score.

and another idea...

* Search the internet to find out how to play 'Shove Halfpenny' and make up a 'Shove Penny' game.
* Polish some pennies and 2p pieces for playing games - if they look really shiny, children will want to play!

Links with the Early Learning Goals

PSRN: Use developing mathematical ideas and methods to solve practical problems.

PSED: Form good relationships with adults and peers. Take turns and share fairly.

Resources and Contacts

Contacts and websites to help develop time and money activities

A few story books to help develop children's understanding of time and money:

> **Night Monkey, Day Monkey** by Julia Donaldson; Egmont Books Ltd
> **The Bedtime Bear: A Pop-up Book for Bedtime** by Ian Whybrow and Axel Scheffler; Pan Macmillan
> **The Very Hungry Caterpillar** by Eric Carle; Puffin
> **What's the Time Mr Wolf?** by Colin Hawkins; Mammoth
> **What's the Time Mr Wolf?** by Annie Kubler; Child's Play
> **Mr Jolly's Joke Shop** by Alan Ahlberg; Puffin Books
> **Funny Bones, the Pet Shop** by Alan Ahlberg; Puffin Books
> **The Great Pet Sale** by Mick Inkpen; Hodder

and there are many more.

Useful websites:

> http://www.canteach.ca/elementary/songspoems4.html This is an American website so watch the terminology and vocabulary!
>
> www.sparklebox.co.uk for downloads of resources and games.
>
> For books, try www.amazon.co.uk and search for children's books featuring the concepts of time and money.

Make sure you use all your local resources:

> the local library service and children's librarian
> your local museum for topic box loans or visits
> parents who may have contacts

The Little Book of Time and Money

The EYFS – Birth to Three

Little Baby Books offer lots of ideas for working with young children, and match the original birth to three framework.

A Strong Child **A Skilful Communicator** **A Competent Learner** **A Healthy Child**

Set 1
978-1-905019-21-2

Set 2
978-1-905019-22-9

Set 3
978-1-905019-23-6

Set 4
978-1-905019-24-3

Also available with the activities grouped according to stage.

Book 1 Heads-up Lookers & Communicators (124pp)
978-1-905019-50-2

Book 2 Sitters, Standers & Explorers (156pp)
978-1-905019-51-9

Book 3 Movers, Shakers & Players (172pp)
978-1-905019-52-6

Book 4 Walkers, Talkers & Pretenders (238pp)
978-1-905019-53-3

All the activities in these books are suitable for the EYFS. Just look for the component and age you need.

To see the full range of Featherstone books visit
www.acblack.com

Continuity and progression

The **Baby & Beyond**™ series takes simple activities or resources and shows how they can be used with children at each of the EYFS development stages, from birth to 60+ months. Each double page spread covers one activity, so you can see the progression at a glance.

Shows how simple resources can be used by children at different ages and stages

Inspiration for planning continuous provision

Messy Play	978-1-905019-58-8
The Natural World	978-1-905019-57-1
The Sensory World	978-1-905019-60-1
Sound and Music	978-1-905019-59-5
Mark Making	978-1-905019-78-6
Construction	978-1-905019-77-9
Dolls & Soft Toys	978-1-905019-80-9
Bikes, Prams, Pushchairs	978-1-905019-76-2
Role Play	978-1-906029-02-9
Finger Play & Rhymes	978-1-906029-01-2
Dens & Shelters	978-1-906029-03-6
Food	978-1-906029-04-3

**To see the full range of Featherstone books visit
www.acblack.com**

through the EYFS

Ideal to support progression and extend learning.

Little Books with *BIG* Ideas®

The Little Book of Painting

Painting isn't just about brushes and powder paint. Painting can go on anywhere, inside or outside, and can involve spraying, splashing, printing, dripping, rolling – and hands!
This Little Book explores an imaginative range of painting activities using different sorts of materials and techniques, encouraging you and the children to experiment. It's beautifully illustrated with the author's own photographs taken in real settings.

ISBN 978-1-9060-2952-4

The Little Book of Story Bags

Story bags are widely used in the Foundation Stage. A story bag contains a focus story book, props and characters to act out the story, plus objects, resources and suggested activities. The idea is to use the story as a springboard to inspire creativity and imaginative role play.

You can buy story bags ready made, but it's also fun to make your own. This book will show you how.

ISBN 978-1-9060-2924-1

Visit our website for more details.
Order now for immediate delivery on publication.